# The People who lived in Burton on Trent in 1864

Compiled by Geoffrey Lindop

MERCIANOTES

Nancy Lindop's The People who lived in Staffordshire part 2

*First published 2010*
*Revised 2015*

Published by:
Mercianotes
Wigton
CA7 5AQ
United Kingdom

© 2015 Mercianotes

ISBN-13: 978-1511616805

ISBN-10: 1511616806

# Contents

# Parishes within 10 miles of Burton

| Parish | mileage | Parish | mileage |
|---|---|---|---|
| Stapenhill | 0.6 E | Church Broughton | 7.3 N by NW |
| Tatenhill | 2.6 W by SW | Chilcote | 7.3 S by SE |
| Stantonand Newhall | 2.8 E by SE | Clifton Campville | 7.5 S |
| Newton Solney | 3.1 NE | Barton Blount | 7.6 N |
| Stanton (Birchover) | 3.1 SE | Dalbury with Lees | 7.6 N |
| Walton-on-Trent | 3.1 SW | Harlaston | 7.7 S by SW |
| Bretby | 3.2 E by NE | Barrow on Trent | 7.8 E by NE |
| Rolleston | 3.2 N by NW | Ashby de la Zouch | 7.8 E by SE |
| Caldwell | 3.2 S by SE | Strettonenle Field | 7.8 S by SE |
| Rosliston | 3.7 S | Sudbury | 8.0 NW |
| Egginton | 3.9 N by NE | Willesley | 8.0 SE |
| Needwood | 3.9 W by NW | Calke | 8.1 E |
| Church Gresley | 4.0 SE | Stanton by Bridge | 8.1 E by NE |
| Marston on Dove | 4.4 N | Trusley | 8.1 N |
| Repton | 4.5 E by NE | Elford | 8.1 S by SW |
| Tutbury | 4.5 N by NW | Mickleover | 8.3 N by NE |
| Barton-under-Needwood | 4.5 W by SW | Kings Bromley | 8.3 W by SW |
| Willington | 4.9 NE | Littleover | 8.4 NE |
| Hartshorne | 5.0 E | Marchington | 8.4 NW |
| Hanbury | 5.3 NW | Thorpe Constantine | 8.7 S |
| Lullington | 5.6 S | Measham | 8.8 SE |
| Etwall | 5.7 N by NE | Melbourne | 8.9 E by NE |
| Wychnor | 5.7 SW | Swarkestone | 8.9 E by NE |
| Blackfordby | 5.9 E by SE | Boylestone | 8.9 N by NW |
| Seal | 5.9 S by SE | Hamstall Ridware | 8.9 W by SW |
| Foremark | 6.1 E by NE | Sinfrin Moor | 9.0 E by NE |
| Netherand Over Seal | 6.1 S by SE | Packington | 9.0 E by SE |
| Findern | 6.2 NE | Packington | 9.0 E by SE |
| Twyford and Stenson | 6.2 NE | Radbourne | 9.0 N by NE |
| Croxall | 6.4 S by SW | Normanton | 9.2 N E |
| Smisby | 6.5 E by SE | Appleby | 9.2 S by SE |
| Edingale | 6.5 S b y SW | Statfold | 9.3 S |
| Foston and Scropton | 6.7 N by N W | Seckington | 9.4 S |
| Yoxall | 6.7 W by SW | Chellaston | 9.5 E by NE |
| Ticknall | 6.9 E | Longford | 9.5 N by NW |
| Ingleby | 6.9 E by N E | Newton Regis | 9.5 S by SE |
| Sutton on the Hill | 6.9 N | Austrey | 9.8 S by SE |
| Alrewas | 7.0 SW | Pipe Ridware | 9.8 W by SW |
| Newborough | 7.1 W by NW | Breedon on the Hill | 9.9 E |

Burton on Trent is distant from London 122½ miles, 33¼ north-east from Birmingham, 25 east from Stafford, 22.5 south-west from Nottingham, 30½ north-east from Leicester, 11 south-west from Derby, 12 north-east from Lichfield, 30 from Stoke and Dudley, 28 from Wolverhampton and Bilston, 64 from Manchester, 89 from Liverpool, 60 from Lincoln, 88 from Leeds, and 52 from Rugby.

# An Eye-witness Account of Burton in 1863

BURTON-UPON-TRENT is a well-built market town of great antiquity, situated in a rich and fertile valley, on the west bank of the Trent, which separates the two shires of Derby and Stafford; The parish is chiefly in the North Offlow hundred, Staffordshire, and partly in Repton and Gresley hundred, Derbyshire, and comprises an area of about 9,000 acres of land. It is divided into seven townships,

- Burton upon Trent, Staffordshire
- Burton Extra, Staffordshire
- Branstone, Staffordshire
- Horninglow, Staffordshire
- Stapenhill, Derbyshire
- Winshill, Derbyshire

The parish is in the diocese of Lichfield, archdeaconry of Stafford, and deanery of Tutbury.

The country round Burton is exceedingly picturesque. East of the Trent the hills slope towards the Ashby Wolds, and from the eminences of Scalpcliff, Winshill, and Bladon, may be seen the valleys of the Trent and Dove, stretched forth in all their beauty. Looking westward across the river, from the same heights, may be seen the Atherstone Out-woods, Needwood Forest, and in the distance the moldering, keep of Tutbury Castle, still frowning defiance from its hill. The aspect of the town itself has been considerably improved during the last fifteen years. The principal streets have had large additions; and breweries, malthouses, and cooperages, all on a scale of unusual magnitude, have been built in an incredibly short space of time.

## A fine Brew

There are few towns in England, or on the continent of Europe, better known than Burton. This celebrity arises from its unrivalled ales. Burton has long enjoyed the just reputation of being the principal place in Europe for the brewing of East India pale and other ales, and such is the demand for them that new breweries are constantly springing up. Great quantities of ale are now exported to every quarter of the globe, which is found to stand the test of every clime. Some idea may be formed of the magnitude of the trade carried on from the fact that the premises of Bass and Co. cover an area of 40 acres, and employ upwards of 1,300 men, and engines of 200-horse power, in their immense breweries, malthouses, cooperages, saw mills, etc. The company are now erecting another brewery of equal magnitude, which will enable them, when finished, to brew 585,000 barrels of ale during the season. The breweries of Messrs. Allsopp and Sons cover an area of 50 acres, and they are about to make very considerable addition to their immense establishment. Burton contains upwards of twenty breweries. Messrs. Salt and Co. have been established upwards of seventy years; their buildings stand upon 5 acres of land, and employ 200 men. The Burton Brewery Company Ltd, have very extensive premises, and are doing a large home and export trade; also Worthington and Sons, and the well-known brewers Ind Coope and Co. at Burton, and Romford, Essex. The London and Colonial Company Ltd have extensive works; and there are many other smaller breweries, which are equally famous for the quality of their ales, including Thomas Robinson, Hill and Sons, John Thompson and Sons, Clement and Berry, London and Burton Brewery Company, Thomas Cooper and Company, John Bell, Joseph Nunneley, Sydney Evershed, and James Eadie.

The other principal trades carried on here are the extensive iron and boiler works of Messrs. Thornewill and Warham, and two small iron foundries, copper works, plaster and cement mills of Messrs. Staton and Company, flint mills, cooperages, etc.

### Road, Rail and Canal
The river Trent, which is navigable for barges up to the town, is crossed by a bridge of great antiquity; it is supposed to have been erected about the time of the Norman accession. A battle was fought on this bridge in 1322 when Edward-II., advancing from Cauldwell, obtained a decisive victory over the Earl of Lancaster; it is now about to be taken down and re-placed by a new one.

The Midland Railway Company have obtained an Act of Parliament to construct a new bridge of 41 arches, which is now (1863) in course of erection, to enable them to make tram-roads by the side of the river to the various breweries. The old bridge has heretofore been kept in repair by the Marquis of Anglesey, but the new one, when completed, becomes the property of the counties of Stafford and Derby, and will be maintained by the two counties. An Act of Parliament was obtained in 1860, by Messrs. Allsopp and Sons, to construct railways to cross the streets of Burton to the various breweries, malthouses, etc., and are now in operation, and cross the streets in many directions.

The Grand Trunk, or Trent and Mersey Canal, communicates with the town and the Trent by a branch at the south end of the town. The Midland (Birmingham and Derby) railway passes west of the town; the station is not large enough to accommodate the increasing wants of the town, though additional buildings have from time to time been raised.

There is a junction here with the North and South Staffordshire, forming a direct route to Manchester and Liverpool, Lichfield, Walsall, Dudley, and the West Midland, and with the Midland line by Ashby-de-la-Zouch to Leicester. Burton thus forms a railway centre.

## Religion

There are three churches. The parish church ( St. Modwen's), stands on the east side of the Market-place; it is a large modern Palladian structure, with little claim to architectural beauty, but it stands in a spacious churchyard, washed on the east by the Trent, on the banks of which some fine weeping willows droop gracefully into the stream: it consists of a nave and aisles, a circular apse or chancel, in which is an altar-piece well executed in white marble, and a tower with eight bells, and a musical set of chimes: in the year 1771 a very good organ was erected in the west gallery. This organ was repaired and improved in 1859, at a cost of £250. The living is a perpetual curacy, value about £200, in the patronage of the Marquis of Anglesey, who is lay impropriator; the Rev. William Jones, M.A.., is the incumbent.

Holy Trinity Church, Horninglow-street, was erected in 1824, at a cost of about £7,000; it is in the florid Gothic style, with a nave, aisles, and chancel, which contain a very beautiful painted window; and it has a highly decorated tower. The living is a perpetual curacy, value £200 yearly, in the patronage of the Marquis of Anglesey, and held by the Rev. Peter French, M.A.

Christ Church, situated in New Street, is a cruciform building, with a lofty spire, in the Early English or lancet Gothic style. The living is a perpetual curacy, value £150 with residence, in the gift of the incumbent of Burton, and is held by the Rev. W. Morgan.

The Independent chapel, in High Street, is a neat, commodious edifice, in the Gothic style, with a lofty front arch.

St. Modwen's Catholic chapel, Guild Street, is a neat brick building, in the Gothic style, with school attached the presbytery, or priest's house, is an elegant and substantial, residence.

The Wesleyan chapel is a spacious and appropriate brick structure, on the northern side of Horninglow Street, fitted up with convenient galleries and pews; attached are neat dwellings for the Ministers.

The Wesleyan Reformers have a very handsome chapel in George Street, a brick building with freestone dressings, with four Corinthian columns in front: it will seat 1,000 persons.

The General Baptists have a neat chapel, a brick building with stone dressings, in Union-street: it will seat 600 persons.

The Particular Baptists have a neat chapel in Station Street: it will seat 500 persons.

The Primitive Methodists have two chapels, one in Station-street, and one in Victoria-terrace. The United Presbyterians have a handsome and spacious chapel in Cross-street: it will seat 800 persons.

## Education

The Free Grammar School, near the parish church, was founded and endowed by William Beane, abbot of Burton, in 1520: a new scheme to extend the staff of masters was in 1858 carried through the Court of Chancery; the Rev.

Henry Day, LL.B., is headmaster; he is assisted by four other masters in the two departments into which the school is divided.

The National schools are situated near Christ church, and are very commodious. New schools for the Trinity church district have been erected in Hawkins Lane by subscription, at a cost of £1,500. The British and Foreign schools are situated in Guild-street.

The Museum, in High-street, is the property of Sir Oswald Mosley, Bart., and contains a good collection of mineral, geological, zoological, ornithological, and other specimens of natural curiosity.

The Literary Societies' rooms, in High-street, have reading and news rooms the library contains upwards of 5,000 volumes.

The Young Men's Christian Association, in Guild Street, have reading rooms, and library containing 4,000 volumes. Three weekly penny newspapers are now published in Burton: *The Chronicle*, on Thursday; *The Weekly News*, on Friday ; and *The Times*, on Saturday.


## Local Government

The Town Hall is in the Marketplace: it was erected in the last century by an Earl of Uxbridge: over the mantelpiece in the hall is a portrait of the late Marquis of Anglesey, of Waterloo renown : in this room are held meetings of business, concerts, public assemblies, etc., but owing to the great increase of the town, a scheme is now under consideration for erecting a new Town Hall and public buildings in another part of the town.

A new town act for Burton-upon-Trent is in operation, and town commissioners, to carry out the same, are elected by the different wards ; John Gretton, Esq ., is the chairman. The County Court House is a handsome Gothic stone building, in Station Street. The Court days are the first Monday in every month. The district comprises:

- Anslow,
- Barton,
- Brimstone,
- Burton,
- Burton-upon-Trent,
- Bretby,
- Castle Greeley,
- Cuffin,
- Cauldwell,
- Church Broughton,
- Church Gresley,
- Coton,
- Drakelow,
- Dunstall,
- Egginton,
- Foston and Scropton,
- Hanbury,
- Hatton,
- Hilton,
- Hoon,
- Horninglow,
- Linton,
- Lullington,
- Marston-upon-Dove,
- Newhall,
- Newton Solney,
- Rolleston,
- Rosliston,
- Repton,
- Stanton.
- Stapenhill,
- Stretton,
- Swadlincote,
- Tatenhill,
- Tutbury,
- Walton-upon-Trent,
- Wichnor,
- Winshill.

Petty sessions are held at the Police station, in Station-street, every Monday.

The Burton-upon-Trent poor law union, formed in 1837, is very extensive, comprising 54 parishes in the counties of Stafford and Derby, viz.:

- Anslow
- Ash (Derby),
- Barton Blount (Derby),
- Barton-under-Needwood,
- Bearwardcote (Derby),
- Branstone,
- Brethy (Derby),
- Burnaston (Derby),
- Burton Extra,
- Burton-upon-Trent,
- Castle Greeley (Derby),
- Catton (Derby),
- Cauldwell (Derby),
- Church Broughton (Derby),
- Church Greeley (Derby),
- Coton-in-the-Elms (Derby),
- Dalbury with Lees (Derby),
- Drakelow ( Derby),
- Dunstan,
- Egginton (Derby),
- Etwall ( Derby),
- Findern (Derby),
- Foremark (Derby),
- Foston and Scropton (partly in Derby),
- Hanbury,
- Hargate,
- Manor (Derby),
- Hatton (Derby),
- Hilton (Derby),
- Hoon (Derby),
- Horninglow,
- Ingleby (Derby),
- Linton (Derby),
- Lullington (Derby),
- Marston-upon-Dove (Derby),
- Mickleover (Derby),
- Newton Solney (Derby),
- Osleston and Thurwaston (Derby),
- Radbourne (Derby),
- Repton (Derby),
- Rolleston,
- Rosliston (Derby),
- Stanton and Newhall (Derby),
- Stapenhill (Derby),
- Stretton,
- Sutton-on-the-Hill (Derby),
- Swadlincote (Derby),
- Tatenhill,
- Trusley (Derby),
- Tutbury,
- Twyford and Stenson (Derby),
- Walton-upon-Trent (Derby),
- Wichnor,
- Willington (Derby)
- Winshill (Derby).

**Miscellaneous**
The market day is Thursday; and there are four annual fairs: Oct. 29 Candlemas-day, April 5, and Holy Thursday. There is also a statute fair for the hiring of servants on the Monday after Michaelmas-day. The town is governed by a high bailiff, who is also coroner. This office is filled by John Richardson, Esq.; Mr. William Coxon is town clerk.

The Self-supporting Dispensary, near the Market-place, was established in 1830. For the small weekly payment of a penny for each individual, or fourpence for a family, it affords medicine and surgical aid to the poorer inhabitants.

Burton now musters three companies of volunteers, amounting to 250 officers and men.

Burton contains three banks and a savings bank:

- The Burton, Uttoxeter and Ashbourn Union bank, in High-street;

- The Derby and Derbyshire Bank, High-street;

- The London, Birmingham and South Staffordshire, Horninglow-street;

- The Savings Bank, in High-street, was established in 1818, and reinstituted in 1842 ; Mr. William Coxon is secretary.

The workhouse is a large and substantial red-brick building, ornamented with stone, situated in Horninglow Street; the cost of erection was £8,200. But few vestiges of the noble old Abbey still remain. The remains of the entrance gate and porter's lodge still exist, opposite the end of New Street. In the Abbey gardens, a beautiful doorway was discovered a few years since, ornamented with carving of the most elaborate execution. Here are almshouses for 15 poor women, and several other small charities.

The total population of the parish and its townships amounted in 1861 to 16,824 ; while the total population, of the town (which includes Burton borough, Burton Extra, and a portion of Horninglow township) amounted in the same year to 13,671.

WETMOOR lies to the north. Henhurst is 1 mile and a half west. The Marquis of Anglesey is Lord of the Manor, and principal landowner.

# Private Residents Directory

## A

Adams, Mr. Edmund, 129 Station Street
Allsopp, Hen. esq. J.P. 181 Horninglow St
Anderson, Mr. John, Bond Street
Atterbury, Mr. James, Branston Road
Atterbury, Mr. James, sen. 81 High St

## B

Barrett, Mr. William, 49 High Street
Bass, Abraham, esq. Moat bank
Bass, Michael Arthur, esq. High Street
Baxter, Mr. Benjamin, 105 Horninglow St
Belcher, Paul, esq. 8 Guild Street
Belcher, Robert Shirley, M.D., Lichfield St
Bell, Mr. John, Lichfield Street
Bottinger, Mr. Hy. 167 Horninglow St
Bradbourne, Rev. Charles Randall, B.A.
    [curate], Lichfield Street
Brown, Edwin, esq. Union bank, High St

## C

Causton, Rev. Edward. Atherton, B.A.,
    101 Moor Street
Clark, Mrs., 180 High Street
Clarke, Mr. Henry, 13 Market place
Coleman, Rev. William Henry, M.A.,
    High Street
Cooper, Miss, 61 Lichfield Street

## D

Day, Rev. Henry, LL.B., Lichfield Street
Delap, Rev. Andrew Bredin, 101 Moor St
Dilworth, Mr. Richard, 130 Station St
Drewry, James, esq. 45 High Street
Drewry, William John, esq. 45 High St

## E

Earp, Mr. Thomas 178 Horninglow St
Evershed, Mr. Sydney, Lichfield Street
Farmer, Mrs. Brooks Buildings

Field, W. Nutt, esq,. 25 Horninglow St
Finlay, James, esq. The Abbey
Ford, Mr. Ham Qrandley, Lichfield St
French, Rev. Peter, M.A.,
    175 Horninglow Street

## G

Gilbert, Mrs. 20 Guild Street
Goer, Mr. Thomas, 18 High Street
Goodger, Henry, esq., Lichfield Street
Greaves, George, esq., 180 High Street
Gretton, John, esq. 61 High Street
Guilding, Edwd. Winfleld, esq.,
    Victoria House

## H

Harris, Mr. Edward, Branstone Road
Hawkins, Mr. Hen., 190 Horninglow St
Healey, Mr. John, Branstone Road
Higginson, Arthur, esq., Station Street
Hodson, Mr. Henry, 120 Station Street
Holbray, Rev., George [Wesleyan],
    151 Horninglow Street
Hutton, Alexander, esq., High Street

## J

Jennings, Edward Billett, esq.,
    Trent Cottage
Jones, Rev., William, M.A. Lichfield St

## K

Kenney, Rev. Rd. [Baptist], Branstone rd
Kettle, Rev. George, Branstone Road

## L

Lathbury, Mr. Joseph, 176 High Street
Lathbury, Miss, 124 Station Street
Lathbury, Misses, 2 Carlton Villas
Lowe, Geo. esq. M.R.C.S., 5 Horninglow St

## M

Martin, Mr. William Shubrick, The Firs
Mason, William, esq., 99 Horninglow St
Meakin, Mr. Francis Lewis, Abbey St
Moore, Miss, 121 Station Street
Morgan, Rev. William, B.A., Church St

## N

Nadin, Mr. Joseph, Hunters Lodge
Newton, Mr. William, Shobnall Road

## O

Oldish, Mr. Walter, Branstone Road
O'Reilly, Rev. Charles James, BA.,
    182 Horninglow Street

## P

Parsons, Fredk. Joseph, esq. Bridge St
Payne, Mrs. 78 High Street
Perks, John, esq. Burton Extra
Pitt, Rev. Alexander, Moor Street
Port, Mr. Francis, Bond Street
Poyser, Josiah Thomas, esq.148 High St.
Prince, William Taylor. esq. 104 High
    Street  and at Repton, Derbyshire
Proudman Mr. John, 5 Carlton Villas

## R

Ratcliff, Mr. James, 6 Horninglow St
Ratcliff, Richard, esq. Lichfield Street
Richardson, Mrs. 60 Lichfield Street
Robinson, Rev. J. H. B.A. [curate],
    Lichfield Street
Robinson, Rev. Wm. Holmes
    [Wesleyan], 152 Horninglow Street
Robinson, Robert, esq. 62 High Street
Robinson, Thomas, esq. 47 High Street
Saunders, Mr. Wm., 180 Horninglow St
Spooner, Thomas, esq., Bridge End
Sproston, John, esq., 181 High Street
Stanley, Mr. William Day, 60 High St
Staton, Mr. John Clarke, Shobnall Road
Styan, Mr. John C., 59 Branstone Road

## T

Telford, Rev. Thomas, B.A.,
    [Roman Catholic], Guild Street
Thomson, Rev., William, Moor Street
Thornewill, John, esq,, Green Street
Tompson, Mr, Frederick James, Station St

## W

Warham, Mr. John R., Orchard Street
Whitehead, Mrs., 151 High Street
Wilkinson, Rev. John,
    [Independent], Moor Street
Wilson, Mitts, Bridge Street
Wyllie, Mr. William, Trent bank

# Commercial Directory

## A

Abbott, Isaac, *beer retailer,* Moor St

Abbott, Thomas, *hairdresser,*
149 Horninglow Street

Ablott, Richard, *glass & china dealer,*
27 Bridge Street

Adams, John & Son, *grocers,* 99 High St

Adams, James, *shoemaker,* 14 Station St

Adams, John, *beer retailer,*
93 Anderstaff Lane

Adams, William, *beer retailer,*
Uxbridge Street

Adams, William, *boot & shoe maker,*
24 Union Street

Allen, Elizabeth (Mrs.), *straw bonnet maker,* 154 New Street

Allsopp, Samuel & Sons, *brewers & maltsters,* High Street

Annable, Mary (Mrs.), *Shopkeeper,*
48 Horninglow Street

Appleby, Henry, *fruiterer,* 4 High St

Appleby, William, *Devonshire Arms,*
83 Station Street

Appleby, William, *shopkeeper,* Station St

Ash James, *furnishing ironmonger,*
1 Market Place

Ash, Thomas, *dispensary,* 178 High St

Atkin, Edward, *Green Man,* 43 New St

Atkin, Sarah (Mrs.), *Shopkeeper,*
43 Horninglow Street

Atkin, William, *butcher,* 100 High St

Atkins, Francis, *commercial traveller,*
George Street

Atkins, Michael, *Midland commercial hotel posting house, coach builder & agent for Croakills agricultural Implements,* Station Street

Auber, Joseph, *watch & clock maker,*
76 Guild Street

## B

Bagnall, Ann (Mrs.), *Furrier,*
208 Station Street

Bagnall, George, *shoemaker & news agent,* 208 Station Street

Bagnall, Richard, *greengrocer,*
21 Guild Street

Bagnall, Thomas, *boot & shoe maker,*
22 Guild Street

Bailey, William, *baker & confectioner,*
104 High Street

Bainbridge, Charles, *Talbot Inn,*
188 Horninglow Street

Ball, James Hamon, *brewers agent,*
102 Station Street

Bamford, George, *greengrocer,*
Victoria Crescent

Banks, Thomas, *fishmonger,*
4 Market Place

Barnes, Abraham, *beer retailer,*
86 New Street

Barrett, William Butler, *gun, pistol & rifle manufacturer,* 48 High Street

Burson, Thomas, *grocer,* Branstone Rd

Bass & Jennings, *solicitors,* 8 Bridge St

Bass Ratcliff & Gretton, *brewers & maltsters,* High Street

Bass Abraham, *solicitor & perpetual commissioner,* Bridge Street
see Burton Cattle Assurance

Bassett, David, *stone & marble mason,*
51 Station Street

Bates, Joseph, *shopkeeper,* 66 Guild St

Batkin, Henry, *cutler,* 25 High Street

Baxter, Nathaniel, *grocer & baker,*
Borough Road

Beard, Charles, *Fox & Goose, licensed to let horses,* 24 Bridge Street

Beck, James, *grocer,* Dale Street

Belcher, Robert Shirley, *physician,*
Lichfield Street

Belcher, Paul, *surgeon,* 8 Guild Street

Belfield, John, *William furniture dealer,* 59A, New Street

Bell, John, *brewer & maltster,*
Lichfield Street

Bell, William, *butcher,* Lichfield Street

Bellamy, Robert Rayner, *bookseller, printer, publisher & proprietor of the Burton Weekly News,* 25 Bridge St

Bennett, William, *whitesmith,* High St

Berry see Clements & Berry

Best & Bowler, *builders* Abbey Street

Bibby, Titus Alexander, *Shakespeare Inn,* Victoria crescent

Binder, Thomas, *supervisor,* 7 Market Place

Bindley, Thomas, *Cooper furnishing & general ironmonger, brazier coppersmith iron & tin plate worker, locksmith, whitesmith, bellhanger, brand cutter, & agricultural implement depot,* 167 High Street

Birch, Henry, *family grocer,* 14 High St

Bircher, George Roes, *Dingo Inn,* Horninglow Road

Bircher, Joseph, *blacksmith,* Anderstaff Lane

Birkin, Chamberlain. *horse breaker,* Lichfield Street

Bissill, Mary (Mrs.), *beer retailer,* 20 Fleet Street

Bladon, Francis Milnes, *Inspector of weights & measures,* 6 Market place

Blunt, Joseph, *grocer,* Wellington St

Blant, Samuel, *shopkeeper,* Moor St

Blood, John, *beer retailer,* Branstone Rd

Blood, John, *shoemaker,* Waterloo St

Bond, William, *New Inn,* 36 Station St

Boothroyd, Charlotte (Mrs.), *ladies school,* Trent Bank

Bosworth, James, *boot & shoe maker,* 54 Station Street

Bowler see Best & Bowler

Bowler, Joseph, *Anchor & brewer,* 5 New Street

Bradbury, Thomas, *coal & hay dealer* 119 Horninglow Street

Bradley, William, *hairdresser,* 132 New Street

Brailsford, John, *soda water manufacturer,* Victoria Crescent

Brandon, Thomas, *farrier & shoeing smith,* 5 Guild Street

Brentnall, Francis, *shopkeeper,* 183 Station Street

Briggs, John Boyd, *plumber etc.* 39 Station Street

Brierley see Cropper & Brierley

Brittain, Joseph, *Tiger,* Hawkins Lane

Brookes, James, *grocer & baker,* 65 Horninglow Street

Brookes, Lydia (Mrs.), *saddler & harness maker,* 122 High Street

Brooks, James, *linen & woollen draper,* 10 High Street

Broster, George, *pork butcher,* 37 High Street

Brown, Edward, *beer retailer & shopkeeper,* 27 New Street

Brown, Edwin see Burton, Uttoxeter & Ashbourn Union Bank

Brown, Joseph, *butcher,* 50 Horninglow St

Brown, Thos *agent for Grand Junction Canal Co.,* Bond End

Brown, William, *agent for Gresley Swadlincote Coal Company,* Railway Coal Wharf

Brunell, Ann (Mrs.), *beer retailer,* Fleet Street

Brunt & Ward, *clothiers & woollen drapers,* 153 High Street

Bryan, Henry, *earthenware dealer,* 3 Bank Square

Bryan, Jesse, *slater,* 104 Anderstaff Lane

Bryan, Mary (Mrs.), *Milliner,* 73 High St

Bryan, William, *butcher,* Moor Street

Burman, Reuben, *shopkeeper,* Hawkins Lane

Burns, William, *beer retailer,* Waterloo St

Burton Brewery Co. Ltd. (William Ferguson manager) High Street

Burton Cattle Assurance Association, (Bass & Jennings, secretaries), Bridge Street

Burton Chronicle, (Joseph Nicholas Tresise proprietor & publisher), Bridge Street

Burton Co-operative Society, *provision dealers,* (John William Flann manager), 15 Guild Street

Burton Times, John Whitehurst proprietor, 163 & 164 High Street

Burton, Uttoxeter & Ashbourn Union Bank, (Mr. Edwin Brown manager, High Street; draw on Roberts, Lubbock & Co. London

Burton Weekly News, Robert Reyner
Bellamy, proprietor Bridge Street
Buxton, Joseph, *shopkeeper*, Mosley St
Buxton, Thomas, *beer retailer,* Berkeley St
Buxton, William, *grocer & baker,* Park St
Buxton, William Moseley, *grocer and
baker,* Waterloo Street

## C

Callant, Thomas, *Old White Lion,*
Lichfield Street
Callingwood, Thomas, *shopkeeper,*
Branston Road
Candland, Martha (Miss), *glass &
china dealer,* 9 High Street
Cantrell, William, *shopkeeper,* 14 New St
Capes, Gabriel, *engineer,* Moseley Works
Capes, George, *linen & woollen
draper,* 3 High Street
Cartmale, Charles, *shoemaker*,
108 Anderstaff Lane
Chambers, Thomas, *beer retailer &
carpente*r Lichfield St
Chambers, William, *Ship.* 19 Bridge St
Chatfield, Dina, (Mrs.), *milliner,*
138 Horninglow Street
Chatterton, Ann (Mrs.), *pawnbroker*,
32 Union Street
Clark, William, *beer retailer,*
18 Horninglow Street
Clarke, William, *builder &
monumental mason,* Burton Bridge
Clarke, William, junior, *bookseller &
stationer*, 175 Station Street
Clayton, Thomas, *wood hoop maker,*
Horninglow Road
Clement, William, *shoemaker,*
8 Hawkins Lane
Clements & Berry, *brewers &
maltsters*, Star Brewery.
Cliff, James, *engineer,* 25 Guild Street
Cliff, Stephen, *shopkeeper,* Uxbridge St
Coates, Henry, *baker,* Lichfield Street
Coates, Samuel, *baker,* 107 High st
Coates, William, *Yorkshire Arms*,
43 Guild Street
Coggins, Eliza (Mrs.), *furrier,*45 Cross St
Collier, William, *shopkeeper*,
Lichfield Lane

Cook, Catherine Jane (Miss),
*ladies school,* Moor Street
Cooke, Elizabeth (Mrs.),
*wine & spirit merchant*,
Bank Square
Cooper, Thomas & Co. *Brewers,*
Horninglow Road
Cooper, Charles, *Wellington Arms,*
Wellington Street
Cooper, John, *hosier & shoemaker*,
52 High Street
Cooper, Stephen, *Spread Eagle,*
106 New Street
Cooper, Thomas, *flint grinder*,
Forge Mill
Corradine, Benjamin, *Malt Shovel,*
41 Anderstaff Lane
Coulton, Josh see Freehold Land
Society
Coxon, James, *accountant,* 63 Guild St,
Coxon, John, *beer retailer,* Moor Street
Coxon, William, *secretary to the
savings bank*, High Street
Cozon, William, *beer retailer,*
Shobnall
Cropper & Brierley, *surgeon dentists,*
High Street
Cross, Thomas, *beer retailer*,
Branston Road
Cubley, Charles, *smith commercial
traveller,* Victoria crescent

## D

Dakin, Joseph, *tailor,* 77 Guild Street
Dalby, William, *carpenter,* 50 Union St
Daniels & Goer, *cheese factors &and
seedsmen,* 18 High Street
Darley, Richard, *bookseller, stationer
and printer* 35 High Street
Day, Lewis, *professor of music*,
Lichfield Street
Dean, George, *boot & shoe maker,*
65 & 66 High Street
Dean, Philip Port, *bootmaker,*
27 Station Street
Denville, Samuel Robinson, *builder,*
Moor Street

Dempster, Thomas, *cabinet maker,*
24 Horninglow Street

Denton, Moses, *tailor,* 32 New Street

Derby & Derbyshire Banking Co.,
(Alexander Hutton, esq manager),
High Street ; draw on Williams,
Deacon & Co Birchin Lane, London

Dickinson & Co., *brewers*; Sun
Brewery Moor Street

Dickinson, Daniel, *boat builder,*
Lichfield Street

Dickinson, John, *grocer, auctioneer &*
*appraiser* 123 High Street

Dilks, Thomas, *grocer,* Wellington St

Dispensary (Thomas Ash, dispenser),
High Street

Doman, Edward, *beer retailer,* Paget St

Douglas, George, *linen & woollen*
*draper,* 86 High Street

Douglas, James, *corn factor,* 17 Station St

Draper, John, *fruiterer,* 156 High Street

Draper, Thomas William, *secretary*
*Literary & Scientific Institution,*
High Street

Drewry, Jas., *solicitor & perpetual*
*commissioner,* 45 High St

Drewry, William John, Jun., *solicitor,*
45 High Street

Dukes, William, *grocer & baker,*
31 New Street

Dulston, John, *shopkeeper,* Paget Street

Dunn, James, *shopkeeper,* 5 Union St

Dunwell, William, *commercial school,*
Anderstaff Lane

Dyche, Mary Ann ( Mrs.), *beer*
*retailer,* Wellington Street

Dyche, William, *beer retailer,*
67 Horninglow Street

Dyer, Charles, *Gas Works manager,*
Anderstaff Lane

E

Eadie, James, *brewer & maltster,* Cross St

Earp, Mary (Miss), *ladies school,*
178 Horninglow Street

Earp, Thomas, *cheesefactors agent,*
178 Horninglow Street

Eaton, John, *shoemaker & town crier,*
215 Station Street

Eley, Joseph, *goods agent London &*
*North-Western Goods Station,*
Horninglow Street

Elliott, Robert Spencer, *tanner &*
*currier,* 68 High Street

Elson, James, *rope & twine spinner,*
42 High Street

Evans, Charles, *travelling draper,*
Hawkins Lane

Evans, William, *grocer & provision*
*dealer,* 29 & 30 High Street

Eaton see Peach & Eaton

Evershed, Sydney, *ale & porter*
*brewer,* Angel brewery

Ewers, Elizabeth (Mrs.), *Milliner,*
155 High Street

Ewers, John, *cooper,* 182 Horninglow St

F

Fairclough, James, *architect &*
*surveyor,* Market place

Feakes, William, *tailor & draper,*
172 Horninglow Street

Ferguson, William see Burton Brewery

Field, W. Nutt, *manager: London,*
*Birmingham & South Staffordshire*
*Bank Ltd.*

Finch, George, *beer retailer,*
Horninglow Road

Firns, Charles, *boat builder & beer*
*retailer,* Shobnall

Fisher, Peter, *beer retailer,* Russell St

Fitchett, Benjamin, *hosier,*
30 Horninglow Street

Fitchett, Henry Simpson, *brushmaker &*
*hardware dealer,* 97 & 98 High St

Fitchett, William, *plumber &*
*paperhanger,* 76 High Street

Fitzsimmons, John, *beer retailer,*
150 New Street

Flann, John William see Burton Co-
operative Society

Fletcher, Catherine (Mrs.), *plumber &*
*glazier,* Lichfield Street

Flynn, Thomas, *greengrocer,* 36 New St

Forbes, Thomas, *Rose & Crown*,
Lichfield Lane
Foster, Henry, *hairdresser & perfumer*,
189 Horninglow Street
Foster, Thomas, *shopkeeper*,
35 Anderstaff Lane
Foster, William, *bootmaker*, 110 High St
Franklin, William, *dyer*, 159 New St
Freehold Land Society's Offices (Josh.
Coulton, sec.), High Street
Froggatt, Thomas, *beer retailer*,
Victoria Crescent

## G

Gene, Frederick, *ironmonger*, 172 High St
Gaskin, William, *plane maker*,
Borough Road
Gas Works (Charles Dyer, manager),
Anderstaff Lane
Gaunt, Thomas, *Union & Railway Inn*,
*& brewer*, 59 Horninglow Street
Geary, William, *shopkeeper*, Orchard St
German, William, *shopkeeper*,
37 Horninglow Street
Gibson, Thomas, *saddler & harness
make*r, 87 High Street
Gibson, William, *currier*, Lichfield St
Gilman, Ellen (Miss), *leather seller*,
17 Market Place
Gilmour, Peter, *beer retailer &
shopkeeper*, Wellington Street
Gimson, Edwd. Atkin, *cabinet maker
& upholsterer*, 82 High Street
Gimson, Henry, *upholsterer, cabinet
maker & paperhanger*, 52 & 53
Station Street
Glenn, Francis, *Builders Arms*,
Moor Street
Glover, Mrs., *straw bonnet maker*,
9 New Street
Glover, William, *wood turner*, 3
George Street
Goer see Daniels & Goer
Goodger, William & Son, f*amily
grocers*, 28 Bridge Street
Goodger, Hen., *solicitor perpetual
commissioner*, Lichfield St
Goodhead, Edward, *shoemaker*,
28 Moor Street

Goodhead, James, *beer retailer*,
108 Station Street.
Goodhead, Samuel, *grocer & baker*,
55 Horninglow Street
Goodman, Caleb, *bookseller, stationer
& news agent*, 74 High Street
Goodman, Mary Jane (Mrs.), *milliner
& straw bonnet maker*, Guild Street
Goodwin, George, *beer retailer*,
Mosley Street
Goodwin, John, *Dog Inn*, and
*hairdresser*, Lichfield Street
Gorton, Thomas, *rate collector*,
1 Mosley Street
Gothard, William James, *tailor &
woollen draper*, 170 High St
Govan, Andrew, *farm bailiff to M.T.
Bass, esq. M.P.* Station St
Grace, Robert, *architect & surveyor*,
131 Station Street
Grand Junction Canal Co. (Thos.
Brown, agent), Bond End
Greaves, George, *surgeon*, 180 High St
Gregory, George Hurst, *cabinet maker*,
53 New Street.
Gresley Swadlincote Coal Co.
(William Brown, agent),
Railway Coal Wharf
Gresley, James, *grocer*, Wellington St
Gretton see Bass Ratcliff & Gretton
Gretton, William, *Carpenters Arms*,
24 New Street
Grimmitt, John, *shopkeeper*, Milton St
Guilding, Edward, *managing partner
London & Colonial Company Ltd*
Gurry, Thomas Musgrove, *shoemaker*,
169 Horninglow Street

## H

Hadfield, John, *beer retailer*, Uxbridge St
Halberd, Phillip F. *ironfounder,
engineer & kitchen range
manufacturer*, Britannia Foundry
Hallam, Chas. Milnes & Francis
*chemists & seedsmen*, 20 High St
Hanson, Thomas, *hairdresser*, 96 High St
Hanson, William, *commercial
traveller*, 89 Guild Street
Hardy, George, *cooper*, Hawkins Lane

Harris, James Kellam, *Provision dealer,* 107 Station Street
Harris, John, *agent:North Staffordshire Railway,* 166 High Street
Harrison, Joseph, *beer retailer & stonemason,* Mosley Street
Harrison, William, *stationmaster Midland Railway Station* Station St
Hatfield, John, *herbalist,* 13 New Street
Hawkins, Henry John & Henry, *linen & woollen drapers and silk mercers,* 191 Horninglow Street
Hawkins, John, *hatter,* 26 Bridge St
Heath, Thomas, *butcher,* 91 High St
Heath, William, *baker,* 142 High Street
Hetford, John, *beer retailer & butcher,* 209 Stations Street
Henchcliffe, Thomas, *tailor,* 67 Anderstaff Lane
Herratt, Samuel, *haberdasher & hosier,* 36 High Street.
Hicklin, John, *tinman,* 23 New Street
Higginson, Arthur, *solicitor,* Station St
Hill, Charles & Son, *brewers & maltsters,* Lichfield Street
Hill, John, *tailor,* 157 New Street
Hill, Mary (Mrs.), *Old Spread Eagle,* Lichfield Street
Hill, Robert, *commercial traveller,* 76 Station Street
Hislop, William Henry, *Stanhope Arms Inn,* 106 Station Street
Hixon, William, *pork butcher,* 157 Horninglow Street
Hodder, Martha (Mrs.), *Shopkeeper,* 20 Horninglow Street
Hodgkins, Joseph, *beer retailer,* Fleet St
Hodson, Henry, *miller,* 14 Market Place
Hudson, William Higgott, *chemist & druggist.* 93 High Street
Hooper, Elizabeth (Mrs.), *Royal Oak,* 9 Market Place.
Hoose, Sarah (Miss), *shirt maker,* 11 Horninglow Street
Hopkins, John, *brewers, agent,* Bridge St
Hopton, James, *furniture dealer,* 51 Union Street
Horne, Thomas, *hairdresser,* 6 High St
Houlden, Richard Thomas, *grocer,* 163 Station Street

Hoult, William, *Saracens Head,* 4 Bridge Street
Hudson, Mary (Mrs), *Angel Inn,* Bank Square.
Hudson, Thomas, *shopkeeper,* 4 Mosley Street
Hudson, William, *grocer & baker,* 154. Horninglow Street
Hunt, William, *cabinet maker & upholsterer,* 72 High Street
Hunter & Bennett, *builders,* Duke St
Hunter, Charles, *shopkeeper,* Moor St
Hurlston, Sarah (Miss), *baker & grocer,* 145 New Street
Hurst, Joseph, *grocer,* 52 New Street

I

Iliff, William, *beer retailer,* Anderstaff Lane
Ind Coope & Co. *brewers & maltsters,* 10 Station Street also at: Romford, Essex, & 10 Osborn Street Whitechapel, London NE
Insley, James, *baker,* 24 High Street

J

Jackson, George, *tailor,* 83 High Street.
Jackson, Thomas, *brazier,* 113 Anderstaff Lane
Jeffcoat, Enoch, *beer retailer,* 30 Cross St
Jeffcoat, William, *shopkeeper,* Cross St
Jefford, Ann (Mrs.), *straw bonnet maker,* 8 Horninglow Street
Jenkins, Thomas, *coal merchant,* Railway Coal Wharf
Jennings see Bass & Jennings
Jerrison, Peter, *slater,* Cross Street
Johnson, John Richd, *greengrocer. & blacksmith,* 11 Station Street
Johnson, Joseph, *beer retailer,* 22 Anderstaff Lane
Johnson, Thomas, *shopkeeper,* Bridge St
Johnson, William, *beer retailer,* Paget St
Jones, Rebecca (Miss), *straw bonnet maker,* 92 High Street
Jones, Thomas, *greengrocer,* Berkeley St
Joule & Parsons, *wine & spirit merchants,* Bridge Street

## K

Kaye, Henry, *grocer*, 88 High Street

Kendrick, Elizabeth (Mrs.), *beer retailer*, 50 Cross Street

Kettle, George McKenzie, *cheesefactor*, 178 Horninglow St

Knight, Frederick, *plumber & glazier*, 105 New Street

## L

Langhein, Theodore, *commercial traveller,* 1 Carlton Villa

Lathbury, Ann (Miss), *milliner & dressmaker,* 154 High Street

Lathbury, Joseph, *tailor*, Horninglow Rd

Lee, Francis, *confectioner.* 2 Bank Square

Lee, John, *butcher*, 165 High Street

Leedam, Wm. &.Son, *grocers & tallow chandlers,* 11 High Street

Leedam, Charles, *pawnbroker,* 182 High Street

Leedam, Francis, *auctioneer*, 42 Union St

Leedam see Stone & Leedam

Leedham, Elizabeth (Mrs.), *shopkeeper*, 11 Lichfield Street

Lees, John Wilton, *Queens hotel,* 3 Bridge Street

Literary & Scientific Institution Secretary: Thomas William Draper, High Street

Lomas, John Woodward, *chemist & druggist,* 168 High Street

London, Birmingham & South Staffordshire Bank Ltd., (W. Nutt Field, esq. manager); draw on head office, 110 Cheapside, London E C

London & Burton Brewery Company Ltd (George Meakin, manager), Abbey Street

London & Colonial Company Ltd, *brewers, maltsters & hop merchants (E. Guilding, managing partner),* Victoria crescent

London & North-Western Goods Station (Joseph Eley, goods agent), Horninglow Street

Lowe, Thomas & Sons, *builders,* Union Street

Lowe, Catherine Ann (Mrs.), *berlin wool & fancy repository;* 165 Horninglow Street

Lowe, George, M.R.C.S. *Surgeon,* 5 Horninglow Street

Low,e Joseph, *rope & twine spinner,* Fleet Street

Lucas, John, *furnishing ironmonger,* 69 High Street

Lynn, Charles, *shopkeeper*, Hawkins Lane

## M

Macpherson, John, *surveyor of taxes,* Lichfield Street

Madeley, Thomas, *Black Horse Inn,* Moor Street.

Mansfield, Samuel, *news agent,* 129 Horninglow Street

Marklew, John, *clothier*, 71 High Street

Marks, William, *shopkeeper*, 51 Cross St

Marlow, Ann (Mrs.), *beer retailer,* 35 Guild Street

Marriott, James, *Welcome Inn*, Wharf

Marriott, Matthew, *clog maker,* 141 New Street

Marshall, Abraham, *grocer,* Victoria Crescent

Marshall, William, *currier*, 42 High St

Martin, John, *tobacconist & news agent,* 33 Station Street

Mason, Henry, *builder*, Guild Street

Mason, Joseph, *grocer*, Lichfield Street

Mason, Joseph, *grocer & baker,* 35 Station Street

Mason, William, *surgeon,* 99 Horninglow Street

Meakin, George, *manager London & Burton Brewery Company Ltd* Abbey Street

Meakin, Henry, *farmer*, Shobnall

Measom, William, *Star Inn, & brewer & maltster*, 152 High Street

Merrey, Charles, *grocer*, Station Street

Merrey, James, *shopkeeper.* 60 New St

Midland Railway Station (William Harrison, stationmaster), Station St

Millward, William, *Lamb*, 90 High St

Milne, Ann (Mrs.), *Wheatsheaf,* 27 High Street

Moore, Charles, *wood turner,* Duke St
Moorcroft, John Clark, *butcher,*
   141 Horninglow Street
Moorcroft, Thomas Charles, *butcher,*
   4 Bank Square
Moorcroft, William, *butcher,*183 High St
Moorcroft, George & Son, *portland*
   *cement & plaster manufacturers,*
   166 Horninglow Street and at
   Kingston Terrace.
Morris, John, *cooper,* 177 Horninglow St
Morris, William, *fruiterer,* 1 High St
Mousley, William & Son, *tailors,*
   Lichfield Street
Mousley, Catherine (Miss), *day school,*
   45 Horninglow Street
Murphy, John, *beer retailer,* Green St

## N

Newbold, George, *painter,* Lichfield St
Newbold, Thomas, *saddler,* 106 High St
Newbould, Robert, *beer retailer,*
   Borough Road
Nichols, Javan, *fruiterer,* 95 High St
Nichols, William, *brewers, engineer,*
   *coppersmith & brass finisher,*
   *plumber, gasfitter etc.* Midland
   copper works, 57 Guild Street
Noon, William, *wood turner,*
   102 Anderstaff Lane
North Staffordshire Railway (Mr: John
   Harris, agent); office, 166 High St
Norton, Elizabeth (Mrs.), *Bootmaker,*
   2 High Street
Nunneley, Joseph, *brewer & maltster,*
   Bridge Street Brewery
Nutt, Henry, *boot & shoe maker,*
   54 New Street
Nutt, Sarah (Mrs.), *milliner &*
   *dressmaker,* 67 High Street
Nutt, William, *grocer & wheelwright,*
   11 Park Street

## O

Ordish & Hall, *linen & woollen*
   *drapers,* 23 High Street
Ordish, Charles *farmer,* Mount Sinai
Ordish, James, *farmer,* 36 Park Street

Orgill, Henry, *tailor,* 105 High Street
Orme, George, *professor of music &*
   *pianoforte & harmonium*
   *warehouse,* 135 High Street, and at
   Sadlergate, Derby
Orme, Thomas, *beer retailer &*
   *saddler,* 165 New Street
Oxford, James, *grocer & baker,*
   55 Station Street

## P

Paine, Alfred, *chemist,* 164 Station St
Parker, Isaac, *basket maker,* 166 High St
Parker, James, *stonemason,*
   53 Horninglow Street
Parker, John, *grocer,* Horninglow Road
Parker, Richard, *baker,* 49 Dale Street
Parker, William, *tailor,* 43 Cross Street
Parry, Peter, *tailor,* 45 Union Street
Patrick, John, *shopkeeper,* 159 Station St
Peach & Eaton, *steam saw mills,*
   Milton Street
Pearson, Margaret (Miss), *ladies*
   *outfitting warehouse,* 85 High St
Perks, Charles & Sons,
   *timber & slate merchants,*
   Lichfield Street
Perks, John, *solicitor,*
   *perpetual commissioner,*
   *commissioner in chancery & all*
   *the common law courts,*
   Burton Extra
Phillips, Richard & Son, *coopers,*
   Borough Road Cooperage
Pickering Brothers, *plumbers,*
   15 Union Street
Pipes, George, *miller,* Borough Road
Port, John Horatio, *hairdresser,*
   3 Market Place
Pountney, William, *chemist &*
   *druggist,* 15 High Street
Power, Charles, *blacksmith,* High St
Poynton, Thomas, *butcher,* 32 High St
Preston, Nathaniel, *glass dealer,* High St
Preston, Thomas, *beer retailer,*
   111 Anderstaff Lane
Price, John, *pawnbroker,*
   16 Horninglow Street

Prince, William Taylor, *solicitor, & commissioner in all the common law courts,* 104 High Street; and at Melbourne

Radford, John, *grocer,* Moor Street

Ratcliff see Bass Ratcliff & Gretton

Ratcliff & Wright, *grocers & druggists,* 102 High Street

Reader, Josiah, *butcher,* 87 Guild St

Redfern, Jane Elizabeth (Mrs.), *milliner,* 179 High Street

Redfern, John, *Coach & Horses,* 84 High Street

Redfern, Thomas, *shoemaker,* 106 High Street

Renwick, James, *shopkeeper,* 73 New St

Reyner, Robert see Burton Weekly News

Richards, Robert, *butcher,* Wellington St

Richardson & Small, *solicitors,* 139 High Street

Richardson, John, *perpetual commissioner,* High Street

Riley, William, *hoop shaver,* 96 Moor St

Roberts, John *pork butcher,* 185 High St

Robinson, George, *shoeing & jobbing smith,* 127 High Street

Robinson, John, *beer retailer,* Branstone Road

Robinson, John, *linen & woollen draper,* 169 High Street

Robinson, John, *professor of music,* Branstone Road

Robinson, Mary (Mrs.) & Helen (Mrs.), *milliners, dressmakers & silkmercers,* 129 High Street

Robinson, Thomas, *brewer,* Station St

Roe, Edward, *carriage builder,* New St

Roe, Edward, *shoemaker,* Wellington St

Roe, Edwin, *baker & shopkeeper,* Moor Street

Roe, Thomas, *hosier & shoe warehouse,* 161 High Street

Rogers, John, *dyer,* 68 Guild Street

Rose, Ann (Miss), *fancy repository,* 21 High Street

Rose, William. *shoemaker.* 12 New St

Rushton, James, *grocer,* Dale Street

Rushton, Samuel, *grocer,* 128 New St

## S

Salt, Thomas & Co. *brewers & maltsters,* High Street

Salt, James, *carrier,* 8 New Street

Sanders, James, *carver & gilder,* 41 Union Street

Saunders, William, *land surveyor & valuer,* Horninglow Street

Savings Bank (Sec: Mr. William Coxon), High Street

Scattergood, Elizabeth (Mrs.), *beer retailer,* Horninglow Road

Shaw, William Greenway, *George family & commercial hotel & posting house,* High Street.

Sheavyn, Samuel, *baker,* 2 Bridge St

Sherwin, Joseph, *watch & clock maker,* 170 High Street

Shotton, Joseph, *grocer,* 39 New Street

Shotton, Joseph, *shopkeeper,* 17 Lichfield Street

Shutes, William, *farmer,* Little Burton

Siddals, Edmund, *general dealer,* 2 New Street

Simnett, Ann (Mrs.), *milliner,* Wellington Street

Simnett, Edward, *butcher,* 1 Bridge St

Simnett, Mary (Mrs.), *servants registry office,* 2 Guild Street

Simnett, Thomas, *shopkeeper,* 48 Anderstaff Lane

Simnett, Wm. *Temperance hotel, & shoemaker,* 154 Station Street

Slater. William, *grocer,* Moor Street

Smalley, Charles, *farm bailiff to J. Gretton, esq.* The Grange

Small see Richardson & Small

Smith, Edmund, *wine & spirit merchant,* 15 Market place

Smith, George, *furnishing ironmonger, brazier & nailmaker,* 56 High St

Smith, Henry, *beer retailer,* Lichfield Lane

Smith, John, *brassfounder,* 192 Station St

Smith, John, *butcher,* 40 New Street

Smith, Robert, *coffee rooms,* 25 Union St

Smith, Robert, *Rising Sun,* 160 Horninglow Street

Smith, William, *wine & spirit vaults*,
192 Horninglow Street
Soar, Thomas, *Plough*,
146 Horninglow Street
Southern, Thomas, *cooper*, 38 High St
Spooner, Thomas, *surveyor, land agent
& accountant*, 179 Horninglow St
Sproston, John, *surgeon*, 181 High St
Staley, Ann (Mrs.), *news agent*,
160 New Street
Staley, Henry, *grocer*, 185 Horninglow St
Staley, William, *beer retailer*, Moseley St
Stanley, Henry, *grocer*,
185 Horninglow Street
Stanley, William, *butcher*, 59 High St
Stanley, William, *house decorator*,
46 High Street
Staton, John Clarke & Co.
*manufacturers of roman & portland
cements, blue lias, lime, plaster of
paris, floor plaster, gypsum for
manure etc.*, Bromley Road.
Steer, Henry, *watchmaker & optician*,
19 High Street
Stone & Leedam, *blacksmiths*, Alfred St
Stratford, Richard, *Guild tavern*,
24 Guild Street
Stratton, John, *builder*, Lichfield Street
Straw, Emily (Miss), *Nags Head*,
Lichfield Street
Stretton, Eliza (Mrs.), *Coopers Arms*,
11 Anderstaff Lane
Stretton, William, *beer retailer*,
62 Cross Street
Styan, John Christopher, *linendraper*,
101 High Street
Sutherns, Ann & Sarah (Misses),
*dressmakers*, 61 Horninglow Street
Sutherns, Thomas, *cooper*, 38 High St
Sutherns, William, *beer retailer*,
Orchard Street
Sutton, William, *fishmonger*,
13 Station Street
Swindale, William, *wine & spirit
vaults*, Abbey Street

T

Tait, Camilla (Mrs.), *Bell Inn*, 166
Horninglow Street

Talbot, William, *shopkeeper*, Lichfield St
Taylor, Charles, *beer retailer*, 73 Guild St
Taylor, Thomas, *chemist & veterinary
surgeon*, 54 High Street
Thacker, John, *Bridge Inn*,
Little Burton
Thompson, John & Son, *pale ale etc.
brewers, & maltsters*,
183 Horninglow Street
Thornewill & Warham, *ironfounders &
engineers*, 18 New Street
Thornewill, John, *solicitor,
commissioner in chancery & all the
common law courts*, Police office,
Station Street
Timms, Thomas, *grocer*,
125 Horninglow Street
Tipper, William, *shoemaker*, Paget St
Tong, John, *umbrella maker*, 26 High St
Townsend, William, *chemist &
druggists* 120 High Street
Tresise, Joseph, *printer & publisher of
the Burton Chronicle;* Station Street
Tricklebank, Thomas, *tailor*, Mosley St
Tull, Charles, *Bear Inn*, 186 Horninglow St
Tunnadine, Henry, *wood hoop maker*,
64 Horninglow Street
Turner, James & Son, *plumbers,
painters & glaziers, & gasfitters*,
70 Guild Street
Turner, David, *beer retailer*,
Victoria Crescent
Turner, James, *beer retailer*, 9 Union St

U

Underwood, Thomas, *provision dealer*,
75 High Street

V

Vanderweyer, Casemere, *beer retailer*,
Dale Street
Virtue, William, *beer retailer*,
15 Lichfield Street

W

Wain, Joseph, *tailor*, Moor Street

Walker, Henry William, *commercial traveller,* 127 Horninglow Street

Walker, William, *coal dealer,* Railway Coal wharf

Walker, William, *linen & woollen draper,* 8 High Street

Walker, William, *shopkeeper,* 151 Horninglow Street

Walters, Thomas, *news agent,* New St

Ward see Brunt & Ward

Ward, Arthur Henry, *saddler & harness maker,* 177 High Street

Ward, Elizabeth (Mrs.), *beer retailer & nail maker,* Abbey Street

Ward, Sarah (Mrs.), *baker & grocer,* Fleet Street

Ward, William, *shoemaker,* 37 New St

Wardle, William, *boot & shoe make*r, 103 High Street

Wardle, William, *nurseryman & seedsman,* Station Street

Waterson, Thomas, *grocer,* 114 Anderstaff Lane.

Watson, John, *general dealer,* 158 New St

Watson, Joseph, *haberdasher,* 23 Guild St

Wayte, John, *grocer & wine merchant,* 7 High Street

Wayte, William, *provision dealer,* 184 Horninglow Street

Webb, John, *tailor,* 94 High Street

Webb, John, *shopkeeper,* Victoria Crescent

Webster, George, *gasfitter,* 184 High St

Wheeldon, Samuel, *beer retailer,* Park St

Wheatcroft, John Nuttall, *commercial traveller,* 4 Carlton Villas

Whitby, Francis, *Boot,* 109 High Street

Whitehead, James, *boot & shoe maker,* 2 Market Place

Whitehead, Sarah (Mrs.), *Butcher,* 156 High Street

Whitehurst, John, *printer, bookseller, stationer & publisher of the Burton Times, & postmaster,* 163 & 164 High Street

Whitford, William, *hairdresser,* 141 High Street

Whittingham, John, *provision dealer, poulterer & confectioner,* 160 High St

Whittingham, John, jun. *Grocer,* 159 High Street

Wigley see Wileman & Wigley

Wilders, Henry, *cork merchant,* Trent Bank

Wileman & Wigley, *builders,* 82 Horninglow Street

Wilkins, Stephen, *auctioneer & upholsterer,* 22 High Street

Williams, William, *carver & gilder,* 70 Station Street

Wiltsher, Sarah & Ann (Misses), *milliners,* Orchard Street

Wilson & Co. *millers,* Burton Mill

Wilson, George, *shopkeeper,* Victoria Crescent

Wilson, John, *fishmonger,* 89 High St

Wilson, Richard, *Staffordshire Knot,* Station Street

Wilson, Thomas, *clock & watch maker,* 44 High Street

Winfield, William, *Bowling Green Inn,* Railway Station

Winfield, William, *King of Prussia,* 153 New Street

Wood, Jane Eleanor (Mrs.), *White Hart commercial hotel,* High Street

Wood, William, *Barley Mow,* 24 Park St

Woodman, George, *beer retailer,* Waterloo Street

Woodroffe, David & Henry, *drapers & outfitters,* 174 & 175 High Street

Woolerton, Joseph, *shoemaker,* 131 Horninglow Street

Woolley, Frances (Mrs.), *White Horse,* 157 High Street

Worsey, Thomas, *grocer & provision dealer,* 13 High Street

Worthington & Sons, *brewers & maltsters,* 47 high Street

Worthington, William & Sons, *distillers & wine merchants,* 144 High Street

Worthington, Thomas, *clock & watch maker,* 111 High Street

Wright, Edwin, *engineer,* 51 Horninglow Street

Wright, Joseph George see Y.M.C.A.

Wright, Mary (Mrs.), *milliner & dressmaker,* 126 High Street

Wright, William, *grocer &
    confectioner,* 155 Station Street
Wright see Ratcliff & Wright

## Y

Yates, Charles, *professor of music,*
    110 Horninglow Street
Yealey, Ludwick, *watch & clock
    maker,* 34 High Street
Yeomans, Handel, *shopkeeper*
    Horninglow Road
Yeomans, John, *brewer & maltste*r,
    50 High Street
Yeomans, Mary (Mrs.), *Blue Posts,*
    50 High Street
Young Mens' Christian Association
    (Joseph George Wright, librarian),
    Guild Street

# Classified Directory

## Accountants
Coxon James
Spooner Thomas

## Agencies
Atkins Michael
Brown, Thos
Brown William
Eley Joseph
Harris John
Hopkins John, brewers

## Appraisers
Dickinson John

## Architects
Fairclough James
Grace Robert.

## Auctioneers
Dickinson John
Leedam Francis
Wilkins Stephen

## Bakers
Bailey William
Baxter Nathaniel
Brookes James
Buxton William
Buxton William Moseley
Coates Henry
Coates Samuel
Dukes William
Goodhead Samuel
Heath William
Hudson William
Hurlston Sarah (Miss)
Insley James
Mason Joseph
Oxford James
Parker Richard
Roe Edwin
Sheavyn Samuel
Ward Sarah (Mrs.)

## Basketmakers
Parker Isaac

## Beer Retailers
Abbott Isaac
Adams John
Adams William
Barnes Abraham
Bissill Mary (Mrs.)
Blood John
Brown Edward
Brunell Ann (Mrs.)
Burns William
Buxton Thomas
Chambers Thomas
Clark William
Coxon John
Cozon William
Cross Thomas
Doman Edward
Dyche Mary Ann ( Mrs.)
Dyche William
Finch George
Firns Charles
Fisher Peter
Fitzsimmons John
Froggatt Thomas
Gilmour Peter
Goodhead James
Goodwin George
Hadfield John
Harrison Joseph
Hetford John
Hodgkins Joseph
Iliff William
Jeffcoat Enoch
Johnson Joseph
Johnson William
Kendrick Elizabeth (Mrs.)
Marlow Ann (Mrs.)
Murphy John
Newbould Robert
Orme Thomas
Preston Thomas
Robinson John
Scattergood Elizabeth (Mrs.)
Smith Henry
Staley William
Stretton William
Sutherns William

**Beer Retailers** - contd
Taylor Charles
Turner David
Turner James
Vanderweyer Casemere
Virtue William
Ward Elizabeth (Mrs.)
Wheeldon Samuel
Woodman George

**Bellhangers**
Bindley Thomas Cooper

**Blacksmiths**
Bircher Joseph
Johnson John Richd
Power Charles
Stone & Leedam
*see smith, shoeing*

**Boat Builders**
Dickinson Daniel
Firns Charles

**Booksellers**
Bellamy Robert Rayner
Clarke William, jun.
Darley Richard.
Goodman Caleb
Whitehurst John

**Bootmakers**
Adams William
Bagnall Thomas
Bosworth James
Dean George
Dean Philip Port
Foster William
Norton Elizabeth (Mrs.)
Nutt Henry
Wardle William
Whitehead James
*see also shoemaker*

**Brand Cutter**s
Bindley Thomas Cooper

**Brass Finishers**
Nichols William

**Brassfounders**
Smith John

**Braziers**
Bindley Thomas Cooper
Jackson Thomas
Smith George,

**Brewers**
Allsopp Samuel & Sons
Bass Ratcliff & Gretton
Bell John
Bowler Joseph
Burton Brewery Co. Ltd
Clements & Berry
Cooper Thomas & Co.
Dickinson & Co.
Eadie James
Evershed Sydney
Gaunt Thomas
Hill Charles & Son
Ind Coope & Co.
London & Burton Brewery Co. Ltd
London & Colonial Company Ltd
Measom William
Nunneley Joseph
Robinson Thomas
Salt Thomas & Co.
Thompson John & Son
Worthington & Sons
Yeomans John

**Brewers Agents**
Ball James Hamon

**Brewers Engineers**
Nichols William

**Brushmakers**
Fitchett Henry Simpson

**Builders**
Best & Bowler
Clarke William
Denville Samuel Robinson
Hunter & Bennett
Lowe Thomas & Sons
Mason Henry
Stratton John
Wileman & Wigley

**Butchers**
Atkin William
Bell William
Brown Joseph
Bryan William
Heath Thomas
Hetford John
Lee John
Moorcroft John Clark
Moorcroft Thomas Charles
Moorcroft William
Poynton Thomas
Reader Josiah
Richards Robert
Simnett Edward
Smith John
Stanley William
Whitehead Sarah (Mrs.)

**Butchers, Pork**
Broster George
Hixon William
Roberts John

**Cabinet Makers**
Dempster Thomas
Gimson Edwd. Atkin
Gimson Henry
Gregory George Hurst
Hunt William

**Carpenters**
Chambers Thomas
Dalby William

**Carriage Builders**
Roe Edward

**Carriers and Couriers**
Elliott Robert Spencer
Gibson William
Marshall William
Salt James

**Carvers & Gilders**
Sanders James
Williams William

**Cheese Factors**
Daniels & Goer
Kettle George McKenzie

**Cheesefactor's Agents**
Earp Thomas

**Chemists**
Hallam Chas. Milnes & Francis
Hudson William Higgott
Lomas John Woodward
Paine Alfred
Pountney William
Taylor Thomas
Townsend William
*see also dispensaries and druggists*

**Clock & Watch Makers**
Wilson Thomas
Worthington Thomas

**Clog Makers**
Marriott Matthew

**Clothiers**
Brunt & Ward
Marklew John

**Coach Builders**
Atkins Michael

**Coal Dealers**
Bradbury Thomas
Walker William

**Coal Merchants**
Jenkins Thomas

**Coffee Rooms**
Smith Robert

**Commercial Travellers**
Atkins Francis
Cubley Charles
Hanson William
Hill Robert
Langhein Theodore
Walker Henry William
Wheatcroft John Nuttall

**Confectioners**
Bailey William
Lee Francis
Whittingham John
Wright William

**Coopers**
Ewers John
Hardy George
Morris John
Phillips Richard & Son
Southern Thomas
Sutherns Thomas

**Coppersmiths**
Bindley Thomas Cooper
Nichols William

**Cork Merchants**
Wilders Henry

**Corn Factors**
Douglas James

**Cutlers**
Batkin Henry

**Dealers, Earthenware**
Bryan Henry

**Dealers, General**
Siddals Edmund
Watson John

**Dealers, Glass & China**
Ablott Richard
Candland Martha (Miss)
Preston Nathaniel

**Dealers, Hardware**
Fitchett Henry Simpson

**Dealers, Hay**
Bradbury Thomas

**Dealers, Provision**
Burton Co-operative Society
Evans William
Harris  James Kellam
Underwood Thomas
Wayte William
Whittingham John
Worsey Thomas

**Dentists** - *see Surgeon Dentists*

**Dispensaries**
Ash Thomas
*see also Chemists and Druggists*

**Distillers**
Worthington William & Sons

**Drapers**
Feakes William
Woodroffe David & Henry

**Drapers, Linen**
Brooks James
Capes George
Douglas George
Hawkins Henry John & Henry
Ordish & Hall
Robinson John
Styan John Christopher
Walker William

**Drapers, Travelling**
Evans Charles

**Drapers, Woollen**
Brooks James
Brunt & Ward
Capes George
Douglas George
Gothard William James
Hawkins Henry John & Henry
Ordish & Hall
Robinson John
Walker William

**Dressmakers**
Lathbury Ann (Miss)
Nutt Sarah (Mrs.)
Robinson Mary (Mrs.) & Helen (Mrs.),
utherns Ann & Sarah (Misses)
Wright Mary (Mrs.)

**Druggists**
Hudson William Higgott
Lomas John Woodward
Pountney William
Ratcliff & Wright
Townsend William
*see also Chemists and Dispensaries*

**Dyers**
Franklin William
Rogers John

**Engineers**
Capes Gabriel
Cliff James
Halberd Phillip F.
Thornewill & Warham
Wright Edwin

**Fancy Repositories**
Rose Ann (Miss)

**Farm Bailiffs**
Govan Andrew
Smalley Charles

**Farmers**
Meakin Henry
Ordish Charles
Ordish James
Shutes William

**Farriers & Shoeing Smiths**
Brandon Thomas

**Fishmongers**
Banks Thomas
Sutton William
Wilson John

**Flint Grinders**
Cooper Thomas

**Fruiterers**
Appleby Henry
Draper. John
Morris William
Nichols Javan

**Furniture Dealers**
Belfield John William
Hopton James

**Furriers**
Bagnall Ann (Mrs.)
Coggins Eliza (Mrs.)

**Gasfitters**
Nichols William
Turner James & Son
Webster George

**Glaziers**
Fletcher Catherine (Mrs.)
Knight Frederick
Turner James & Son

**Greengrocers**
Bagnall Richard
Bamford George
Flynn Thomas
Johnson John Richd
Jones Thomas

**Grocers**
Adams John & Son
Baxter Nathaniel
Beck James
Birch Henry
Blunt Joseph
Brookes James
Burson Thomas
Buxton William
Buxton William Moseley
Dickinson John
Dilks Thomas
Dukes William
Evans William
Goodger William & Son
Goodhead Samuel
Gresley James
Houlden Richard Thomas
Hudson William
Hurlston Sarah (Miss)
Hurst Joseph
Kaye Henry
Leedam Wm. &.Son
Marshall Abraham
Mason Joseph
Merrey Charles
Nutt William
Oxford James
Parker John
Radford John
Ratcliff & Wright
Rushton James
Rushton Samuel

**Grocers** - contd
Shotton Joseph
Slater. William
Staley Henry
Stanley Henry
Timms Thomas
Ward Sarah (Mrs.)
Waterson Thomas
Wayte John
Whittingham John, jun.
Worsey Thomas
Wright William

**Haberdashers**
Herratt Samuel
Watson Joseph

**Hairdressers**
Abbott Thomas
Bradley William
Foster Henry
Goodwin John
Hanson Thomas
Horne Thomas
Port John Horatio
Whitford William

**Hatters**
Hawkins John

**Herbalists**
Hatfield John

**Hoop Shavers**
Riley William

**Hop Merchants**
London & Colonial Company Ltd

**Horse Breaker**
Birkin Chamberlain.

**Horse Letters**
Beard Charles

**Hosiers**
Cooper John
Fitchett Benjamin
Herratt Samuel
Roe Thomas

**House Decorators**
Stanley William

**Inspectors Of Weights & Measures**
Bladon Francis Milnes

**Iron & Tin Plate Workers**
Bindley Thomas Cooper

**Ironmongers**
Ash James furnishing
Bindley Thomas Cooper
Gene Frederick
Halberd Phillip F.
Thornewill & Warham

**Ironmongers, Furnishing**
Lucas John
Smith George,

**Land Agents**
Spooner Thomas

**Land Surveyors & Valuers**
Saunders William

**Leather Sellers**
Gilman Ellen (Miss)

**Locksmiths**
Bindley Thomas Cooper

**Maltsters**
Allsopp Samuel & Sons
Bass Ratcliff & Gretton
Bell John
Clements & Berry
Eadie James
Hill Charles & Son
Ind Coope & Co.
London & Colonial Company Ltd
Measom William
Nunneley Joseph
Salt Thomas & Co.
Thompson John & Son
Worthington & Sons
Yeomans John

**Manufacturers**
Barrett William Butler

**Manufacturers** - contd
Brailsford John
Halberd Phillip F.
Moorcroft George & Son
Staton John Clarke & Co.

**Masons**
Bassett David
Clarke William
Harrison Joseph
Parker James

**Merchants, Timber & Slate**
Perks Charles & Sons

**Millers**
Hodson Henry
Pipes George
Wilson & Co.

**Milliners**
Bryan Mary (Mrs.)
Chatfield Dina (Mrs.)
Ewers Elizabeth (Mrs.)
Goodman Mary Jane (Mrs.)
Lathbury Ann (Miss)
Nutt Sarah (Mrs.)
Redfern Jane Elizabeth (Mrs.)
Robinson Mary (Mrs.) & Helen (Mrs.),
Simnett Ann (Mrs.)
Wiltsher Sarah  & Ann (Misses)
Wright Mary (Mrs.)

**Nail Makers**
Smith George,
Ward Elizabeth (Mrs.)

**News Agents**
Bagnall George
Goodman Caleb
Mansfield Samuel
Martin John
Staley Ann (Mrs.)
Walters Thomas

**Newspapers**
Burton Chronicle
Burton Times.
Burton Weekly News

**Nurserymen**
Wardle William

**Opticians**
Steer Henry

**Outfitters**
Woodroffe David & Henry

**Painters**
Newbold George
Turner James & Son

**Paperhangers**
Fitchett William
Gimson Henry

**Pawnbrokers**
Chatterton Ann (Mrs.)
Leedam Charles
Price John

**Perfumers**
Foster Henry

**Physicians**
Belcher Robert Shirley
*see also surgeons*

**Plane Makers**
Gaskin William

**Plumbers**
Briggs John Boyd
Fitchett William
Fletcher Catherine (Mrs.)
Knight Frederick
Nichols William
Pickering Brothers
Turner James & Son

**Posting Houses**
Atkins Michael
Shaw William Greenway

**Postmasters**
Whitehurst John

**Poulterers**
Whittingham John

## Printers
Tresise Joseph
Bellamy Robert Rayner
Darley Richard.
Whitehurst John

## Professors Of Music
Orme George
Day Lewis
Robinson John
Yates Charles

## Public Houses
Bowler Joseph
Hudson Mary (Mrs)
Wood William
Tull Charles
Tait Camilla (Mrs.)
Madeley Thomas
Yeomans Mary (Mrs.)
Whitby Francis
Winfield William
Thacker John
Glenn Francis
Gretton William
Redfern John
Stretton Eliza (Mrs.)
Appleby William
Bircher George Roes
Goodwin John
Beard Charles
Shaw William Greenway
Atkin Edward
Stratford Richard
Winfield William
Millward William
Corradine Benjamin
Atkins Michael
Straw Emily (Miss)
Bond William
Hill Mary (Mrs.)
Callant Thomas
Soar Thomas
Lees John Wilton
Smith Robert
Forbes Thomas
Hooper Elizabeth (Mrs.)
Hoult William
Bibby Titus Alexander
Chambers William

Cooper Stephen
Wilson Richard
Hislop William Henry
Measom William
Bainbridge Charles
Simnett Wm.
Brittain Joseph
Gaunt Thomas
Marriott James
Cooper Charles
Milne Ann (Mrs.)
Wood Jane Eleanor (Mrs.)
Woolley Frances (Mrs.)
Coates William

## Publishers
Bellamy Robert Rayner
Bellamy Robert Rayner
Whitehurst John
Tresise Joseph

## Rate Collectors
Gorton Thomas

## Rope & Twine Spinners
Elson James
Lowe Joseph

## Saddlers & Harness Makers
Brookes Lydia (Mrs.)
Gibson Thomas
Newbold Thomas
Orme Thomas,
Ward Arthur Henry

## Schools, Commercial
Dunwell William

## Schools, Day
Mousley Catherine (Miss)

## School, Ladies
Boothroyd Charlotte (Mrs.)
Cook Catherine Jane (Miss)
Earp Mary (Miss)

## Seedsmen
Daniels & Goer
Hallam Chas. Milnes & Francis
Wardle William

**Servants Registry Office**
Simnett Mary (Mrs.)

**Shirt Makers**
Hoose Sarah (Miss)

**Shoeing & Jobbing Smiths**
Robinson George

**Shoemakers**
Adams James
Adams William
Bagnall George
Bagnall Thomas
Blood John
Bosworth James
Cartmale Charles
Clement William
Cooper John
Dean George
Eaton John
Goodhead Edward
Gurry Thomas Musgrove
Nutt Henry
Redfern Thomas
Roe Edward
Rose William.
Simnett Wm.
Tipper William
Ward William
Wardle William
Whitehead James
Woolerton Joseph
*see also bootmaker*

**Shopkeepers**
Annable Mary (Mrs.)
Appleby William
Atkin Sarah (Mrs.)
Bates Joseph
Blant Samuel
Brentnall Francis
Brown Edward
Burman Reuben
Buxton Joseph
Callingwood Thomas
Cantrell William
Cliff Stephen
Collier William
Dulston John

Dunn James
Foster Thomas
Geary William
German William
Gilmour Peter
Grimmitt John
Hodder Martha (Mrs.)
Hudson Thomas
Hunter Charles
Jeffcoat William
Johnson Thomas
Leedham Elizabeth (Mrs.)
Lynn Charles
Marks William
Merrey James
Patrick John
Renwick James
Roe Edwin
Shotton Joseph
Simnett Thomas
Talbot William
Walker William
Webb John
Wilson George.
Yeomans Handel

**Silk Mercers**
Hawkins Henry John & Henry
Robinson Mary (Mrs.) & Helen (Mrs.)

**Slaters**
Bryan Jesse
Jerrison Peter

**Smith**
Cubley Charles
*see blacksmith, whitesmith, coppersmith*

**Smiths, Shoeing**
Brandon Thomas

**Solicitors**
Bass & Jennings
Bass Abraham
Drewry Jas.
Drewry William John, Jun.
Goodger Hen.
Higginson Arthur
Perks John

**Solicitors** - contd
Prince William Taylor
Richardson & Small
Thornewill John

**Stationers**
Clarke William, jun.
Darley Richard.
Goodman Caleb
Whitehurst John

**Steam Saw Mills**
Peach & Eaton

**Straw Bonnet Makers**
Allen Elizabeth (Mrs.)
Glover Mrs.
Goodman Mary Jane (Mrs.)
Jefford Ann (Mrs.)
Jones Rebecca (Miss)

**Supervisors**
Binder Thomas

**Surgeons**
Belcher Paul
Greaves George
Lowe George, M.R.C.S.
Mason William
Sproston John
*see also Veterinary Surgeons*

**Surgeon Dentists**
Cropper & Brierley

**Surveyors**
Fairclough James
Grace Robert.
Spooner Thomas

**Surveyors Of Taxes**
Macpherson John

**Tailors**
Dakin Joseph
Denton Moses
Feakes William
Gothard William James
Henchcliffe Thomas

Hill John
Jackson George
Lathbury Joseph
Mousley William & Son
Orgill Henry
Parker William
Parry Peter
Tricklebank Thomas
Wain Joseph
Webb John

**Tallow Chandlers**
Leedam Wm. &.Son

**Tanners**
Elliott Robert Spencer

**Tinmen**
Hicklin John

**Tobacconists**
Martin John

**Town Criers**
Eaton John

**Umbrella Makers**
Tong John

**Upholsterers**
Gimson Edwd. Atkin
Gimson Henry
Hunt William
Wilkins Stephen

**Veterinary Surgeons**
Taylor Thomas

**Warehouses, Ladies Outfitting**
Pearson Margaret (Miss)

**Warehouses, Pianoforte & Harmonium**
Orme George

**Warehouses, Shoe**
Roe Thomas

**Watch & Clock Makers**
Auber Joseph
Sherwin Joseph

**Watch & Clock Makers** - contd
Steer Henry
Yealey Ludwick

**Wheelwrights**
Nutt William

**Whitesmiths**
Bennett William
Bindley Thomas Cooper

**Wine Merchants**
Wayte John
Worthington William & Sons

**Wine & Spirit Merchants**
Cooke Elizabeth (Mrs.)
Joule & Parsons
Smith Edmund

**Wine & Spirit Vaults**
Smith William
Swindale William

**Wood Hoop Makers**
Clayton Thomas
Tunnadine Henry

**Wood Turners**
Glover William
Moore Charles
Noon William

# Also available from Mercianotes

**The People who lived in Staffordshire:**

1.  Hanley

2.  Burton-on-Trent

**Nancy Lindop's Genealogies:**

1.  Lindop

2.  Hampton and Grindley

3.  Baker, Furnival, Jones and Shuker

For further details please visit:

**www.mercianotes.com**

www.ingramcontent.com/pod-product-compliance
Lightning Source LLC
Chambersburg PA
CBHW070524290526
45790CB00003B/1285